MADE IN VERMONT

PHIL STANNARD

MADE IN VERMONT

Copyright © 2017 by Phil Stannard
All rights reserved.

ISBN Number: 978-1-60571-393-9

Cover Photo: Author's grandfather and his prized team, Jack and Joe, dressed in their "work gear."
Back Cover Photo: Stockwell/Bartley family early Vermont settlers

Printed in the United States of America

TO MY BEST CHILDHOOD FRIEND , "RICKY," RICHARD H. BEEBE, JR.
(May 20, 1946-March 13, 2017), who passed away 18 days prior to my completion of this book. His spirit inhabits these Vermont woods

AND

TO MY WIFE KATHY, FIVE CHILDREN, PHIL-MIKE-NATHAN-BRETTE-LORIEN, GRANDCHILDREN AND LARGE EXTENDED FAMILY,
all of whom remain here, working to preserve the work ethic, spirit, character and history of this unique place called Vermont.

CONTENTS

INTRODUCTION i

CHAPTER ONE Summer Vacation 1

CHAPTER TWO Vermont Life...8

CHAPTER THREE The Town That "Was"................................14

CHAPTER FOUR Choices...28

CHAPTER FIVE Religious or Spirtual 32

CHAPTER SIX Andy...37

CHAPTER SEVEN Like Father Like Son.................................42

CHAPTER EIGHT Flight History..54

CHAPTER NINE Flight History of the World 58

CHAPTER TEN Snake Country 63

CHAPTER ELEVEN Tribute to Patriots..................................66

CHAPTER TWELVE Beaurocratic Socialism 73

REFERENCES 80

CHAPTER THIRTEEN Fun with Pictures..............................81

MADE IN VERMONT

INTRODUCTION

I DECIDED TO WRITE THIS BOOK, not because there is anything notable about my story, but rather about a place and time in history through which I have lived, that not enough is written about. It may one day be considered one of the two or three most significant periods of Vermont and its influence on a nation. The period from 1945 to 2016 represents the entire rise, reign, and early decline of Vermont as a significant industrial/agricultural mecca, a complete metamorphosis of its character to a caricature and numerous other political and economic conditions. I like to say that "as goes Vermont, so goes the country," first to free slaves, aggressive in producing and protecting the country's independence, and liberties, notable at the forefront of the development of an independent nation, with Ethan Allen and The Green Mountain Boys, and General George J. Stannard leading the Vermont Boys in the Civil War at Gettysburg. I'll talk about a religion here that developed into a worldwide movement.

In modern times, beginning with Gov. Madaline Kunin, Vermont has completely reversed its political image from tough defenders of freedom, liberty and independence to leading the nation in its decline into "Bureaucratic socialism," not equaled or joined by the nation until the election of President Barack Obama. As a news commentator, Bill O'Reilly has often chided Vermont as a liberal laughing stock. As a noted historian, Bill O'Reilly should have looked deeper into the people and events that shaped, and ultimately re-shaped this interesting place, and where it fits into the unapologetic experiment called America. He should have explained where the blame lies, and how it all fits into the equation of repeated history. He didn't do that, so I will. I have lived all of it. In setting the stage for analyzing this period, I will also refer to the events and attitudes and experiences of some of my many ancestors who in other times were more interesting and influential than I, and had a great deal to do with the founding and development of this great place.

CHAPTER ONE

SUMMER VACATION

MY EYES OPEN QUICKLY AND WIDE to the realization that summer vacation starts right now. Bedroom windows are open and the sounds and smells of summer of 1957 are clear and motivating. A noticeable knot in my stomach from the 14 hot dogs and quart of cherry Kool-Aid at yesterday's school picnic give me pause. Outside my open bedroom windows, the sounds of hundreds of crow's nervous callings are almost deafening, but doesn't drown out the loud clanging of milk cans being unloaded by area farmers onto the conveyer at the creamery across town, or the banging of rail cars being hooked up at one of the town's half dozen or so rail sidings. Quarry whistles start blowing on the outskirts of town. It must be 7:00 am, time for hundreds of workers to start their day of mining and milling slate. This little town brags of being "The slate capital of the world."

So much to do! So much to experience! So many places to go! So much to explore! Ricky and I agreed to get summer started at 7:30 am. I'd better get going!! I make the stairs in three long bounds, bouncing off the wall in the hallway at the bottom, charge past my parents at the breakfast table and through the kitchen door onto the porch. There it is! Three Maplewood Dairy bottles of milk delivered by Charlie Dailey. I run back into the house with them, grab the cream stopper and a bowl of cheerios. After I insert the stopper into the bottle, I pour the heavy cream off the top of the bottle onto my cereal. Wow, life is good! That half pint of cream will fuel my day, and who knows, maybe my future!

Time to run! As I charge back out the door, mom hollers, "Where you going?"

"Out Mom!"

"When are you coming back?"

"Later!!" I race to the end of the driveway, just in time to see Ricky running down the street after me. I hesitate, then run across the street to make Mrs. Field's front door ahead of him. As I throw open her screen door without knocking, and land one foot onto her shiny hardwood floor, I hear that beautiful sound. "Come in boys! I was expecting you! I'm in the kitchen!"

I had smelled the baked goods from the front porch, a mixture of heavenly odors that I can recall even now, sixty years later. Donuts, breads, cookies, pie. Wow, again, life is good! Ricky grabs cookies. I ask for a slice of peach pie, and of course, milk is served with both.

After an in-depth discussion about our plans for the summer, and some hurried advice about everything from heat stroke to lightning, we give her a quick hug, a thank you, and race again to the front door.

Bill Barsalow has moved his bakery off Willard Avenue to Main Street, downtown, and in addition to being our best customer for night-crawlers and fish worms all summer, he has offered us some work at the bakery. So we'll head downtown, with a quick run through Cordelia's kitchen door to grab a couple more treats on our way. She hollers a greeting in that friendly, high pitched voice, and asks us not to forget to take care of her lawn!

Immediately, at the bakery, Bill picks on us for being late and points to a large pile of pans in the pot sink that need scrubbing. We scrub, wash, and put away for more than an hour, amidst constant and humorous heckling from Bill and Dick as they trim out massive amounts of baked goods and bread behind us. Bill gives us each two buffalo nickels and tells us to stop out front at the dairy bar counter so Arlene can properly award us with ice cream and honey glazed donuts. Unaware of our two previous stops, she picks on us for being able to put it all away. My God, life is good!!

Time to run again, down the sidewalk, next door, to Hastings Shepard's Store. We paw through today's assortment of bubblegum flat packs to see which baseball cards we want to add to our collections, or attach with clothes pins to our bike wheels, to make motor noises throughout the neighborhood later in the day. We pick out two each and give Hastings our nickels. This early in summer, the selection is great! Maybe we should go mow a couple of lawns and get back here, "Better hurry boys, they're selling like hot cakes!"

My dad meets us on the sidewalk on his way to his coffee break at the diner, from the bank.

"Hey dad, will you give us a ride to Bill Wood's field after dark tonight? Bill Barsalow wants 200 nite crawlers, and we need to buy baseballs."

"Sure! If you get all your chores done and show up on time for dinner."

"We'll be there! See ya!"

Seeing Dad reminds me of stories he tells about being a kid growing up in the nineteens and twenties. Born in 1910, he was raised on the family farm, two miles outside town and rode behind a team on a buckboard with his dad, into town to the family owned grist mill in 1920, on his first day of summer vacation. "Father" he said, "was proud of his team. He relaxed the reins and let the horses plot along as if totally indifferent about the trip. It seemed to take forever, until they reached the edge of town. Somewhere between Ed Reed's and "Pickle" Enos' houses, he started clicking sounds and some light rein slapping. The team picked up the signals quickly and with no further coaxing, lifted their heads and tails and pranced fancily through town, proud as hell, with timed synchronized, hoof beats, and harness gear jingling. Ahead of him was a day of bagging grain, greasing hubs, dressing belts, climbing around in the rafters shooting rats, and running errands around town. In cold winter weather, that ride into town was no joke. When dad was cold, grandfather kicked him off the wagon, to run along behind it until he was warm again.

MADE IN VERMONT

View of The Grist Mill from the Main Street level.

-Mirror Image from below the Dam- Grandfather Stannard's Grist Mill at the foot of Main Street Hill on the Dam in Fair Haven.

When making winter trips out of the lumber camp back to the sawmill across from the farm with a sleigh full of logs, Grandfather kicked dad off the sleigh at the top of the icy Bigelow Hill, arched his back into the seat top with feet firmly planted on the spiked foot break levers on each side of the sled and instructed the horses to begin the descent. One careful step after the other, driving spiked shoes into the ice, runners squeaking and brakes scraping. They worked together to safely descend the 200 yards to the bottom of the steep, ice covered road. One little miss-step or mistake, bad timing, a broken brake or horse shoe, and the lives of all but dad were at risk. Only when grandfather rested the reins and horses at the bottom and whistled for dad, was he allowed to sit down and slide to the bottom. Life was precious and precarious, but good!

Suddenly that spell is broken by a loud, sharp holler as Hastings calls us back to the store. Must have a delivery for us. Well close. "Hey boys, take this bag to Phil's grandmother. She just called and my delivery truck is already out.

The first day of summer is ripping by too quickly, but we'll find time for bike riding, whiffle ball, BB guns, and catching bees in a jar on the Mountain Pink bush in Ricky's front yard. Maybe tomorrow we'll make it down to the town dump to shoot rats with our 22's, or run down to the river just above the dump for some trout fishing. Life is busy, but good!

I often wonder what many folks' grandchildren will write about in 60 years. We spent our lives outdoors. Many of them spend most of theirs indoors. We wandered throughout the town in daylight and darkness, on foot, or bicycles, unattended. In many places now, they get picked up by DSW if they wander 1/4 mile from home, and their parents are cited by police for neglect. We hunted, fished, trapped, built go carts and rode them without helmets, up and down the streets and roads of town, also unattended. They ride bikes, four wheelers, and such, in body armor and helmets, under strict supervision, and on boring designated trails. We rode on our dad's lap at the age of 6, going down the highway, learning to steer and operate the car. They ride, strapped into a car seat, in the back seat, staring at the ceiling and the back of the front seats. We ate three meals a day with our families, where we learned manners, respect, social skills and how to live our lives safely and respectfully, and plan them, with other people included. They eat soda, snacks, gluten free, sugar free, nut free, fat free, nourishment free processed foods out of drive-up window, fast food bags in their rooms with their doors shut so they won't be scolded for discarding the kale garnish. We weren't allowed to use the "party line" phone on the wall without permission. They spend their entire lives texting, face-booking, snap-chatting, tweeting, sexting, etc. to such a degree that their posture is affected by bending over looking constantly at their latest "device." Much of the difference between their way of life and ours is progress, some of it not, and 21st century kids should be advised against trying much of our 1950's lifestyle at home. Millennials have much more at their disposal than we did, and can benefit by what they make of it. At the same time, much of the improved safety and increased opportunities in their lives, are overshadowed by the dangers posed by increased populations, negative changes in social behavior and terrorism.

Our lives were good, and I'm sure if you ask millennials in 2076, many will tell you the same. They'll write about it, and about folks like us from affectionately interesting, and humorously outdated earlier times.

CHAPTER TWO

VERMONT LIFE

VERMONT IS A SMALL STATE in both population and area, but the greatness or significance of a state is not measured by either. In its beginnings Vermont was settled by the toughest, most determined people in America. They were ready to enter significant conflicts to protect the territories and their nation. Their productive outburst in agriculture and industry surpassed all surrounding settlements.

Early on, Vermont's rich crop of timber was cleared to create open crop land to grow and supply hay to the cities of New England, while the lumber business flourished as part of America's new construction. Vermont supplied some of the best lumber, ship building lumber and timbers, ship masts, finished lumber for furniture and all other things wooden and of stone. Once cleared the land was kept open by sheep, as demand for wool flourished. Then with the invention of the "horseless carriage," hay and sheep crops declined and the forests started creeping back in.

Then to the 1930's when stricken with disease, financial desperation, helplessness, and facing the possibility of some sort of revolt, folks fled the cities for the survival qualities of rural America. Places like Vermont, once again, took on hardy, resourceful populations of pioneers, and industry and agriculture continued to flourish here through WWII. Machine tooling, tool and die making, stone mining, furniture making, commercial agriculture, and industry and commerce in general grew and flourished. Folks in the cities began to do well financially and soon became vacation travelers curious about that little green state with all the mountains and lakes, pastoral farms, village greens and church steeples. They came here to vacation and air out the kids. Soon the kids, spoiled by a rich life and some pampering, rushed back here in Volkswagen micro busses and made over camper vans, beginning in the 1960's to that beautiful place they remembered visiting, to escape the draft, career boredom, and other sober realities. They cleared little one or two acre patches at the back of old farms now owned by their wealthy parents and began building tee-pees, communes, and outhouses. They grew pot, parsley, and pickled peppers, and fed their babies goats milk. They sold the cheese, free range chickens, eggs and herbs roadside and home schooled their kids. By the 1970's they were growing well-trimmed beards or wearing pretty flowers in their hair, sewing cute patches on the elbows of their sport coats and smoking aromatic tobaccos in sophisticated looking curved stemmed pipes.

First, they became teachers and then soon began to take over the legislature without firing a shot, and the transformation from Vermont's character to a caricature had begun in earnest. Somewhere in my young adult life, as a fully aware native, surrounded by a strong family, hardworking friends and a greater sense of community values, I survived the transformation and took on the fight against it, a battle lost and a certain way of life not saved.

I travelled the state fighting hard against Act 250, Vermont's "death of development" law. I fought against zoning and so-called "planning," and then "regional planning," statewide control of education, utilities and natural resources. The culmination of my life long lost battle against these freedom robbing, counter productive transformations led me finally to a run for the state's highest office in the year 2000. I despised then Governor Howard Dean and the extreme damage caused by him to the state that I felt could take a generation or more to repair, physically and financially. I was wrong. A generation later, it's worse, not better. Realizing that both parties were stuck in gridlock and acceptance of the "status quo." I ran as an "Independent." Now in 2016, that might have worked, but this state wasn't ready for it in 2000. I lost and realized that in fact, Vermont was still raising sheep, but the sheep where wearing clothing.

When my father was born in 1910, Vermont was the home of 32,909 family farms, a vibrant manufacturing climate up and down the rivers, and a healthy industry involving the forests and its resources. It generated all of its own electricity, maintained full scale rail and shipping services, and was capable of employing all of its youth. Lake Champlain was a busy shipping waterway. In my town of

Fair Haven, more slate was mined and more roofing and industrial slate and tiles produced per area than anywhere else in the US. In the immediate area of our town more than twice the slate was produced than in all the other states in the union. The first slate quarry in Fair Haven was opened in 1839. Fair Haven is the center of the area that produces unfading green, purple and mottled slates. Fair Haven has manufactured nails, plywood, newsprint, paper, clocks, clothing, synthetic nylon products, marbleized slate products and much more.

Fair Haven / West Haven (once one in the same) thrived in agriculture and forestry as a result of its' proximity to Lake Champlain, railroads, highways, low sea levels and rich soils. This lower Champlain valley is a unique place, noted for species and climate characteristics common as far south as Pennsylvania. A breed of timber rattlesnakes from that southern region makes Fair Haven its' northern most home. Southern species of trees have crept their way up this Champlain valley that don't exist anywhere else in Vermont or the Adirondacks. Fair Haven sits fairly flat in the belly of this beautiful, arid, and fertile valley at only about 300 feet above sea level. It remains the convergence of major rivers, roads, rail, and shipping routes representing the rugged face of industry and commerce that made this state and the country the best this world had to offer after WWII.

Here I was living this amazing occurrence, eating the fruits, feeling the freedoms, contemplating the opportunities. I was walking it, seeing it, smelling it, feeling it. Surely it could never end! Life was good! Life was precious! Surely it would go on forever.

Unknown climber atop Welcome to Fair Haven sign on October 17, 1917.

Mining slate the hard way early in the 20th Century.

Steamers Ticonderoga and Vermont at dock on Lake Champlain, Burlington.

CHAPTER THREE

THE TOWN THAT "WAS"

SINCE MUCH IS MADE on these pages of the rise and fall, the grit and toil and history of this place, I think the reader will find it interesting to read the summary of Fair Haven's assets, as appeared in a local article of *The Fair Haven Record* in 1896. 120 years ago, the town was growing and booming, and the people gathered in the streets and meeting halls regularly to express their pride and celebrate the town.

Following the announcement that the Bell Foundry of Boston Mass, would locate to Fair Haven and employ 150 people, another article described the excitement and celebration downtown. The article was titled "The Booming of the Cannon." The sub heading read "Ringing of Bells, Burning of Fireworks, and General Rejoicing mark the Inauguration of the New Era."

Ringing of Bells, Burning of Fireworks, and General Rejoicing Mark the Inauguration of the New Era.

Friday evening was a noisy one in Fair Haven after the announcement was made that the stock for the bell company had all been subscribed. Never doing things by halves its business men were prepared and the firing of cannon, the burning of fireworks and the ringing of the bells became general throughout the town. For an hour Green's Block was ablaze with colored fire and other illuminations and the small boy was in his element. Nearly everyone knew at once by the noise that the bell concern was to be located here, but some rushed down town under the impression that there was a fire raging. One old gentleman came to the center the following morning and inquired "what the celebration was over?" On being told that it was the bell factory he sniffed in disgust and remarked "well, I'll be god darned! I thought Cleveland was dead."

Our people will stand all the noise the boys can make on such an occasion as this.

Downtown Fair Haven in 1900.

Downtown Fair Haven in 1950.

Fair Haven, Vermont Hotel Allen.

MADE IN VERMONT

Fair Haven, Vermont United Shirt and Collar Co's. Factory.

2 miles north of Fair Haven on West Haven Road (now Route 22A) lies Smith's Tavern (AKA Halfway House) 1780-1903 visited by the "famous" and the "infamous" in their travels between Vergennes and Bennington-Manchester area from the Revolution to 1903. Author's grandfather Stannard burned the Tavern and replaed it with his own homestead on same location in 1903.

Stock wagons waiting in line for Depot access (1800s).

It is known that the celebration went on for days, and included excitement of other industries and new construction of improved water power facilities. To quote my great grandfather around that time, "The town is healthy, and living cheap!"

As a result of the exuberance of the entire town another article is as follows, printed in its entirety:

> *The country feels gratified, the town of fair haven is proof and the village is nearly wild over the bright prospects of this fair municipality for the future. No town blessed as ours with bright, intelligent and enterprising citizens can be kept back and then great truth has been exemplified in the past week by truthful facts not to be denied. And our people are not stopping at this one success. They propose to go further*

and the work of the past few days is to be continued until Fair Haven can claim the honor of being the leading manufacturing town of the state.

Just at this time it is interesting to bring together the present industries of Fair Haven and see what we really already have, look back and see what built up our town to its present magnitude, to see wherein Fair Haven has been successful, to find precedents that will make it easier to make further successes.

And other successes can be made.

Of course it is a well-known fact that the main industry of Fair Haven is slate, and to slate the town largely owes its success. The following are the slate concerns of Fair Haven.

ROOFING SLATE

    Eastern Slate Co.
    E. D. Humphrey
    E. E. Lloyd Slate Co.
    W. E. Lloyd Slate Co.
    New Empire Slate Co
    Valley Slate Co.
    Eureka Slate Co.
    Evergreen Slate Co.

One or two of the quarries of the above concerns are located on the Fair Haven Poultney line but can well be considered as Fair Haven industries as the managers are residents and leading citizens of this town.

The following are mill owners or marbleizers:

    S. Allen & Co.
    Bonville Bros.
    Cooperative Slate Co.
    Coulman & Westcott
    Fair Haven Marble and Marbled Slate Co.
    Durick & Keenan.
    Hazard Slate Co
    Maley Bros.
    M. Maley.
    McNamara Bros.
    W. H. Pelkey.
    Welsh Cooperative Slate Co.
    Edward Bonville.
    A. B. Young.

Robert Jones & Co.
Wm. Francis & Co.
Roberts & Owen.

These 25 concerns are all doing good business from year to year and represent a large amount of capital.

OTHER INDUSTRIES

As stated above the main industry is slate but there are many other manufactories that add to the general prosperity of the place, as follows:

E. R. Hill, wagons and sleighs.
Union Carriage Shop.
Champlain Valley Creamery.
Green Bros, patent, medicines, and extracts
O. A. Peck, furniture.
John Foy, harness.
W. E. Ripley, harness.
W. C. Crippen, flour and feed.
E. H. Phelps, flour.
Glass Granite Works, monuments.
Jacob Warner, monuments.
E. Prunier, confectionery.
C. T. Maynard & Co, machinery.
E. W. Jones, clothing.
C. O. Benson, wood.
H. K. Sheldon, lumber.
Wallace Bros, laundry.
W. H. Pelkey, machinery.
George Dalrymple, tubing.

MERCHANTS

Fair Haven has the reputation of being the trade center of a large surrounding country and has magnificent stock of goods which are second to none in the State. The following is a list of the merchants, all of whom are entering upright in deal and honorable in all their transactions.

Carl Hughes, stationary.
Williams & Metcalf, boots and shoes.
S. D. Williams & Son, boots and shoes
H. T. Jones, general merchandise.

New York Dry Goods Store, dry goods.
John Powell, dry goods.
Charles Sterns & Co, dry goods.
E. Prunier, confectionery.
Bardy, Wilsong & Root, clothing.
Norton, Pollard & Carmody, clothing.
E. W. Jones & Sons, merchant tailors.
Rolland C. Reed, lumber and coal.
D. R. Williams, coal.
Green Bros, clothing.
G. E. Adams, drugs.
W. C. Crippen, meal, feed, etc.
O. A. Peck, furniture.
Hughes Bros, clothing.
E. W. Bailey, groceries.
Thomas McGuire, groceries.
Peck the Grocer, groceries.
Preston Bros, groceries.
J. M. Ryan, groceries.
F. H. Shepard, groceries.
C. W. Sutliff, groceries.
Norton Hardware Co. hardware.
J. H. Foy, harness.
W. E. Ripley, harness.
W. F. Parker, jeweler.
M. Stoinert, jeweler.
Maley Bros, meats.
Fox & McGourty, meats.
M. A. Hayes, millinery.
B. N. Lloyd & Co., millinery.
E. Maley, millinery.
Miss Murphy & Co., millinery.
E. E. Reynolds, pictures and frames.
J. J. Foley, Mgr., groceries.
Thomas Hughes, boots and shoes.
J. D. Culver, general merchandise.
A. B. Herrington, harness.

These 41 stores are doing prosperous business which speaks highly for the town, and other stores are projected, and the fact that so many exists and prosper is a fitting testimonial to the enterprise of our people and the wealthy of our surrounding towns.

OTHER BRANCHES

For lawyers we have W. H. Preston and George M. Fuller our doctors are A. S. Murray, E. G. Roberts, C. E. Griffin, R. Lape, T. E. Wakefield: insurance is furnished by H, K Sheldon while nearly everybody sells bicycles. Dr. McAllister is a resident optician, while the following attend the duties of the village blacksmiths: W. H. Green, Peter Hope, W. Lincoln, Mr. Falkenbury, Thomas Mitchell. Our local carpenters and builders are N. S. Wood, C. D Leonard, Frank Davis, W. L. Town, J. S. Bosworth, H. W. Farmer. The livery meant are John E. Rutledge, W. K. Merriam and C. W. Crippen & Son, and feed and grain mills are run by W. C. Crippen and B. Merriam. E. E. Reynolds is the photographer and Oa Bryant and the Norton Hardware Co., plumbers. No doubt in the miscellaneous list "there are others" but they will be found under proper heading.

THE CHURCHES

Passing from the commercial features of Fair Haven to its other main ones we naturally come to the churches of the place. A town can be judged by its churches and schools very accurately. And in this connection our readers will be surprised at the number of churches which follow:

St. Mary's Catholic.
Methodist Episcopal.
First Congregational.
First Baptist
French Catholic
St. Luke's Episcopal
Welsh Protestant
Welsh Calvinistic.

The following are the present pastors of the above denominations: St. Mary's, Rev. P. J. Barrett; Methodist, Rev. D. W. Dayton; Congregational, Rev. R. H. Ball; French Catholic, Rev. J. M. Gelot; St. Likes, Rev. W. Parry-Thomas; Welsh Protestant, Rev. John W. Williams; Welsh Calvanistic Rev D. M. Jones. It is necessary for us to comment upon the value of the great influence of these institutions. Upon them depends the welfare of Fair Haven.

THE SCHOOLS

No town in the state is more proud of her schools than Fair Haven. And this especially applies to the graded school which stand at the head. The graded school is under the charge of a board of trustees composed of Charles R. Allen, Dr. A. S. Murray and John T. Powell. The instructors of the institution are as follows:

Principal, W. G. Parks
Assistant Principal, Mrs. L. C. Ruyter
Ninth Grammer, Miss Collins.
Eight Grammer, Miss Edward.
Seventh Grammer, Miss Ryan.
Sixth Intermediate, Miss Leffingwell
Fifth Intermediate, Miss Kinsella.
Fourth Primary, Miss Roberts.
Third Primary, Miss Wood.
Second Primary, Miss Jakeway.
First Primary, Miss Pomeroy.

Nearly 500 pupils are enrolled in the school. The school is a well conducted one of which we may well feel proud. The estimated value of school building and grounds is about $25,000 and they are buildings which are a credit to our entire community.

SECRET SOCIETIES

In all enterprising cities a sociable feeling springs up in the hearts of inhabitants and the reseal tis maternal organizations which are always a source of great pleasure, profit and assistance to the members. Fair Haven has its share and among the leading societies the following have local branches:

Free and Accepted Masons.
Independent Order of Off Fellows.
The Royal Arcanum.
The Royal Society of Good Fellows.
The True Forties.
Grand Army the Republic.
Sons of Veterans.

Enrolled on the membership list of the above organizations is a membership of about 450. All of them are formed for social and benevolent purposes and the amount of good done by each during their existence is hard to compute but it is very great.

THE LIBRARY

If there is any one thing in Fair Haven that is a complete recommendation of our village as a place in which to reside it is the public library. Liberally sustained by the taxpayers and liberally patronized by our people it is an institution that would be a credit to a town ten times as large. It is free to any resident of the place and contains nearly 4,000 volumes covering every field: The present library committee is W. I Howard, E. G. Roberts, D. J. Edwards, Rev P. J. Barrett, F. O, Vaughn, John G. Pitkin, men who take pride in their work and jealously guard the best interest of the institution.

THE FIRE DEPARTMENT

Another attractive feature of Fair Haven and especially to one who contemplates taking up a residence of Fair Haven is one of the most efficient fire departments in New England. There can be no question but that C. C. Knight Hose Co, and the Ira C. Allen Hose Co., are the two best companies of the state. With this assurance new comers will feel more safe, and certainly the low insurance rates for Fair Have will prove an inducement.

FINANCIAL

Fair Haven is blessed with two banks which are solid as the crags of the Rocky Mountains. The town shows strength by the way in which its banking institutions are supported, but so excellent is the management that both depositories are worthy of the trust reposed in them.

The Allen bank was charted in 1879 with a capital of $50,000. Its first president was the lamented Hon. Ira C. Allen, who will always be remembered as one of the leading men of the town and one who done more for the success of his town than any other. The following are the present officers of the Allen National bank: President, S. Allen; vice president, Ira R. Allen; cashier, Charles R. Allen; directors: S. Allen, Ira R. Allen, Charles R. Allen, F. E. Allen, A. Tuttle, Elis Roberts, J. W. Williams.

The First National bank was organized in 1864 with a capital of $100,000. Its present board of officials follow: President, R. G. Abell; vice president. Z. H. Ellis; cashier, W. F. Walker; directors: R. C. Abell, Z. H. Ellis, H. Stannard, A. N. Adams, M. Maynard, F. A. Barrows, H. C. Rumsey.

CARVER FALLS

For years far sighted individuals looked with longing eyes upon Carver Falls as a great water power but it remained for the late James R. Langdon to finally make the move to utilize it, his attention having been called to it by Mr. A Tuttle of this place. The result is that today Fair Haven has the best and most extensive power and lighting facilities in New York or New England. At present power is used from Carver Falls by the Eureka Slate Co., the Fair Haven Shirt Co, the VERMONT RECORD office, the Fair Haven Water Works, by the Stannard farm, A. F. St. Louis' carpet cleaning establishment, the Champlain Valley creamery. Fair Haven as well as Poultney is lit by the current and the enterprise of Fair Haven is shown by the large number of stores, offices and residences that are supplied with light from this magnificent power and lighting station. This plant will always be a great inducement to industries looking for places favorable for a good location. The new factories will probably receive power from Carver Falls.

PLEASANT FEATURES

Many people visit Fair Haven each day and it is a fact that we never met a guest but that he paid Fair Haven high compliments on account of its park, its splendid streets, its pleasant drives, and the beautiful scenery surrounding the town. On the east, Bird mountain rises far above the line of horizon, while back of it, miles away are the bold magnificent peaks of the Green mountains. On the west are the foot hills of the Adirondacks while north and south beautiful fields stretch away to the forests that make a green background to the beautiful picture Fair Haven always presents to the observer. Lake Bomoseen is but a mile and a half away while pleasant drives over smooth well-made roads takes one to Castleton, Whitehall, Lake St. Catherine or Glen Lake with its picturesque surroundings.

Above will be found a list of churches. Connected with them is a large number of

CHURCH SOCIETIES

prominent among which are the Young Peoples' Society of Christian Endeavor, the Epworth League, St. Patrick's Benevolent Union, Ladies Aid, King's Daughters, Ladies Auxiliary besides several minor organizations. Closely allied is the Sound Men's Christian Union which was formed early last winter of which John T. Powell is president. The organization is doing a great amount of good and strangers in town are always welcomes.

Phil Stannard

THE TOWN GOVERNMENT

Of course the success of any town depends, like all other business concerns, upon it management. Both Fair Haven town and village government have always been good but of late years exceptionally superior to many surrounding towns. The following are the offices for the town the coming year:

>Selectmen, O. A. Peck, Ira R. Allen, James Minoque.
>Treasurer, Charles R. Allen.
>Overseer of Poor, O. A. Proctor.
>Constable and collector, W. A. Smith.
>Listers, N. S. Wood, H. S. Humphrey, L. R. S. Griffin.
>Road commissioner, W. H. Streeter Jr.
>Auditors, G. H. Shinville, E. H. Phelps, Jacob Warner.
>Trustee of Public money, R. E. Lloyd
>Grand Jurors, E. E. Lloyd, H. R. Lewis, J. L. Winchell, Humphrey Roberts, O. A. Proctor.
>Inspector of Leather, S. D. Williams.
>Pound keeper, M. W. Kincaid.
>Town Agent to prosecute claims, George M. Fuller
>Cemetery Commissioner, D. R. Williams

THE VILLAGE GOVERNMENT

>The village government is as follows:
>Trustees, D. R. Williams, F. A. Town, H. K. Sheldon.
>Clerk, J. J. Foley.
>Treasurer, C. R. Stevens.
>Collector, W. A. Smith.
>Auditors, G. H. Shinville, W. S. Stevens, E. L. Allen.
>Fire Wardens, T. Leahey, C Connors, G. H. Cobb, H. Decelle, J. J. Brown.

CLUBS

Fair Haven is a social town and as a natural result there are several clubs here, organized on the plan of the leading clubs of the country, where members meet from day to day and discuss business, society news and other interesting topics of the times. These clubs are a feature of the towns progress that should not be overlooked as it more clearly shows the great hospitality of our people.

RAILROAD FACILITIES

No one in Fair Haven claims that the town is a railroad center but we do claim that our railroad facilities are first class. The Delaware and Hudson Canal

Co's road passes through the town and no town so situated has more trains per day than this. New York is but 7 hours.

One can go east or west four times each day. No other road in the country is as liberal as the "D. & H.," and special attention is paid to the business in this section. Freights are quick and shipping facilities can be considered equal to those of Rutland.

TELEGRAPH

Two lines of telegraph cater to the wants of our people, the Postal Telegraph and Western Union. The office of the former is located at the Park View House under the charge of Miss Hermie Lewis and the Western Union is managed by Frank O. Vaughn, Agent for the "D. & H." and the National Express Co.

THE MAILS

Postal facilities are fine. The post-master, W. L. Howard, ably assisted by his son, Herbert H. Howard, has made many improvements in the service and with our numerous mails and centrally located post office everyone should be highly pleased with important branch of Fair Haven's business.

In conclusion let us say that we have now enumerated half the advantages of the town. This article is not intended as a history of Fair Have. It is simply an effort to give people in and out of Fair Haven an idea of what we have, what we have done and what we can do. We hope we have done so. The assurance that we have will be our reward.

Everyone in town was proud, everyone able-bodied was working, and damn it-life was really good!!!

CHAPTER FOUR

CHOICES

IN THAT SUMMER OF MY TENTH YEAR, I was starting to contemplate my future. I thought about every possible occupation and localized lifestyle possible on the land. None of it had anything to do with education. I hated school, and lived for every time the exit bell rang and dumped me back out onto the street to run home as fast as my legs would carry me, to take part in everything that really mattered. Hunting, fishing, trapping, working and playing outdoors, going to the woods with my father, hanging out with friends, and baseball.

In the future, a majority of my friends would choose to focus on education, careers that offered salaries, benefits, vacations, security. A handful of others, and I, would choose the land, the town, and the wild uncertainties of self-dependencies, and the pride associated with the "school of hard knocks." They left. We stayed! They drifted away into corporate America and became part of that on-going "building of America." My best childhood friend, Ricky, disappeared out into that corporate America, seeking the fortunes I couldn't get my head around. We stayed and sought to continue the "building of a vibrant Vermont," a choice that would offer more road blocks and disappointments later in our careers as Vermont went through drastic changes not friendly to native traditions, independent thinking or productivity. We ultimately became the leftovers as "Natives" in the midst of an influx of dreamers, gawkers, and discontents, who would eventually change the landscape and character of this beautiful place. Using laws and regulations they would send the "natives" home to behave themselves, while they placed new labels on everything, shut down the natural resources, regulated liberties and centralized all things to the top of our state government, leaving towns without the autonomy that gave them that strength of character and community they had been famous for. In a failed effort to preserve the character of Vermont, they created a "caricature" of Vermont that was to their liking, and that left real Vermont characters in a helpless passing minority.

Suddenly at some point, I knew what the Native American Indians felt like. They too had once created a balanced and productive system of self-governance and lifestyle that worked well for centuries only to be over-powered and ripped to shreds by a new, self-centered, semi-civilized, onslaught of foreigners whose God apparently forgave them for all of their abuses to others, and calamities of a greedy culture that would change the landscape for centuries to come. In other words, their lives were changed by well-intended, yet wrong-headed foreigners, as were ours. Nevertheless, in 1957 life was very good for us, and now since, our culture and character have been greatly challenged and changed, probably forever.

My ancestors, along with so many others, came here, bravely, to clear this wilderness, and create a productive landscape with which to build a safe haven for their offspring and a better life for themselves.

Nothing civilized existed here before them other than Indian law and very limited Indian settlement. This allows me to argue that I am a true original native of this place and that perhaps all applicable rights should apply. Perhaps I should be able to sell tax free cigarettes and build a casino, with which to extract great sums of money from gawking tourists and greedy middlemen from those other worlds. Perhaps I'm wrong, but no one has argued convincingly against my premise, thus far.

As the imposing Europeans gained superiority of numbers and waring resources over the Indians, the Indians were killed, exiled, portioned onto limited lands and into limited existence, regulated, humiliated, and made to follow customs, laws, and lifestyles not of their choosing. They were left to wander and wonder off into obscurity and oblivion, largely ignored and misunderstood by history. It seems to be the natural order of things. I've seen nothing at all to suggest that there is a difference in the plight of multi-generational Vermonters in recent history, except that the enemy isn't shooting at us yet. It has always been the worst of civilized men that has sought to dominate, regulate, and ruin what is the best and most productive of all the things and people that surround them. It has likewise always been the worst of men to accomplish this by usurping the freedoms and personal liberties of the people they seek to control. As they build and protect their greedy majorities, they create disabled and exiled minorities. Life is always better for some than for others. I have seen, lived and understood it all for seventy years. I studied Indian cultures, languages, wars throughout my high school years and beyond. I felt way back then that Indian struggles would be repeated in history over and over again, and become the similar struggles of other cultures. Early on, I found it easier to relate to the teachings of Black Elk, of the Oglala Sioux, than of Christianity or organized governments. Likewise, I studied, understood and believed the philosophical teachings of Jesus and not the interpretations offered by organized religions.

CHAPTER FIVE

RELIGIOUS OR SPIRITUAL

ONLY ONE ORGANIZED RELIGION, that I am aware of, was started by a gentleman whose teachings, strangely enough mirrored much of my own philosophy, and long before I actually studied his. He was William Miller, a.k.a. Prophet William Miller, founder of the advent movement and Seventh Day Advent. I am his direct descendent.

It has Long been my opinion that organizing religions usurped the accurate interpretations of the leaders they worshipped, or the teachers they held in high regard.

The Catholic religion, perhaps wisely, organized and grew its base following into the largest civilized religion ever known by concentrating on the abstract interpretation of the bible and of Jesus' words. In that early time, this enabled them to gather the struggling masses into organized beliefs that would actually promote structure within a more civilized band of followers led by a government-like structure, bringing people together in a common bond and purpose, and promote some necessary morality, obedience and unity.

William and Lucy Miller.

William Miller was an early and committed scholar of the bible. As a child in a poor rural family, two miles outside Fair Haven in Low Hampton, New York, his parents were unable to provide him with adequate reading material and his curiosity and studies turned to the family bible, where I believe his interpretations led him to espouse an alternative that would develop into the advent movements, that eventually, once again, would take a slightly more abstract approach that would best serve the development needs of their organized following.

I choose to develop my own spiritual/religious beliefs based on my own interpretations of the words and philosophies of Jesus, and respect what I also believe were Miller's similar beliefs, early on.

I am sure that the true followers of any organized religions, including the Advent, would find some disagreement with me, but oddly enough, as I said before, I developed my theories before I studied Miller. Perhaps some inherited generational influence?

Simply put I believe that Jesus was the greatest and most influential philosopher that ever lived. I believe early records claiming that he said, "I am the son of man." I believe the church developed his claim that "I am the son of God," to serve the development of the abstract "father" being, and a disconnected "heaven." I believe he said that "heaven exists here on earth," once again changed to indicate a less definable, mystical abstract.

Jesus had no worldly possessions and was killed before he could organize his following, beyond disciples, to experience the earthly peace and tranquility of that message.

Interestingly enough, Miller did not die first and was able to convince a much larger gathering to dissolve themselves of their worldly possessions and meet on "the rock" a.k.a. "Essention Rock" near his Hampton farm to experience a predicted "second coming of Christ." After Christ failed to show up, and still failing to understand their disillusion of worldly assets or appreciate their new found "heaven on earth," the encampment eventually dispersed to rejoin families and friends, restart their lives and to recalculated the "second coming!"

Miller's wife was not well enough convinced that she was willing to dissolve. Instead she took on Miller's share of the farm and personal belongings, and remained behind. As the story goes, when Miller returned home, knocking at the door, she did not answer. Continued efforts to raise her failed. Finally, after his relentless urgings, she responded, "Who is it?"

He simply replied, "It's William, your husband."

"No, it isn't," she retorted. "William has joined his parishioners on 'the Rock' to meet Jesus and enter heaven."

Eventually a sympathetic Lucy unlatched the door and let him rejoin the family.

Original William Miller Church, located on Miller farm in Hampton, New York just across the border from Fair Haven, Vermont.

"Essentian Rock"-Behind Miller Church located on the Miller Farm.

CHAPTER SIX

ANDY

SOMETIME IN THE SUMMER OF THE TENTH YEAR, I vividly recall playing under the spruce trees in my front yard, where my mother stepped outside the front door and called me inside in a voice that instinctively made me nervous.

I rushed inside to find my brother, mom and dad with long solemn faces at the kitchen table. Dad couldn't speak, so Mom mechanically released the words "Henry called, and said that Andy passed away today." I cried like a baby.

I worshipped Andy. What would I do without my good and trusted friend, Andy?!

Andy seemed like an old man, with his long, fluffy white beard, Santa Clause voice and appearance, and similar jovial presence. He lived in a one room cabin about 8' wide by 12'-14' long with an entry door on the north end, one window on the south end wall, a small wood stove with a single griddle top to the left of the door, then a table and one wooden chair. On the table, always were three things: Crisco lard, peanut butter and bread. Under the table were a sack of flour and a sack of potatoes. I never saw anything else. It was a clean, comfortable and perfect home for a bachelor that spent his life out doors. On the outside of the door was about a 12" by 18" slate with a chalk on a string for messages and beside that, hung a couple of pails, filled with fishing hand lines and tackle. Under the bed was a 22-caliber long rifle with iron sites, he had everything he needed for survival. Andy was a native of the neighborhood, his cabin located on my grandfather's farm, where he was employed in every capacity for I believe his entire adult life. He was born and raised at the foot of Cemetery Hill Road, on the Howard Farm. His family were my families' closest neighbors, in a large Victorian farmhouse just above the Poultney River on the "Old Main Road" that led to a covered bridge across the river above Carvers Falls, into N.Y. state, all part of the then primary route to Whitehall N.Y. The bridge was washed out in the great flood of 1927 and never replaced. The house eventually burned, but the cellar hole remains.

Andy had a lot to do with raising my father and his siblings, fishing, hunting, trapping, rattlesnake hunting and long walks across open rolling Meadows of the farms, berry picking, farm chores, wood cutting, and practical jokes. In my few years with Andy, I learned more about fishing than I ever have since. We'd walk down to the river with a burlap grain sack, hand lines and worms, and always come back with a full sack of bullheads, shad, suckers and pan fish, or trout.

Now I was having my first lesson in "The death of a friend." As hard as it was for me, it must have been really tough on my dad. He spent his entire young life on the farm with Andy, learning the age-old lessons of survival, mostly since forgotten. Stories of the close relationship between the two families, from my dad, were endless following his death,

There was the recounting of a story about Andy's mother known to the family as "Ma" Howard, working with her husband "Doom." Howard in the woods. In the middle of a workday, she delivered a child, wrapped it in a blanket, laid it carefully and comfortably by the brook to keep it calm, and finished the work day before returning home with her new family member.

He spoke about often being a guest at the busy dinner table in the Howard house. After dinner, "Ma Howard gathered the dogs to lick the dinner plates and platters shiny clean, after which they were turned over at their places on the table, ready for the next meal.

Andy was a big rugged man with a gentle demeanor, but a loud clear baritone voice that carried across long distances. My dad always said when he was younger he sounded like Johnny Cash, and in fact sang a couple songs like "Wreck of old 97" that Johnny Cash later made famous. When the kids were little he remembered Andy carrying him and his brother in a "hand basket" over his shoulder on the trips to hunt woodchucks, pick several quarts of berries, or gather rattlesnakes for meat, oil, and a cash "bounty." Rattlers were very plentiful back then and Andy knew everything he needed to know about the "Main Den," the "South den," common scent trails, water holes and "sunning spots." April and September were lucrative hunting months, when snakes were close to dens, leaving or returning.

Andy's brother Jim was a professional rattlesnake hunter and colorful local character, known to everyone. After the fire that took the Howard home, Andy moved into his cabin on our farm and Jim split his time between a similar residence at "Beaver Meadows" near Inman Pond, and a seasonal house boat he used as a working residence on Reed's Marsh, known to locals as "The Mash."

My earliest recollections of Jim were far fewer than of Andy, but worthy of note. He came to our house when we lived in the Village, from time to time. He would knock on the door and greet my mother in the most polite respectful tone you could ever imagine. He would be holding a grain sack full of snakes, usually, but not always dead, and ask "Good morning Mrs. Stannard, it's a pleasure to see you. Is Mr. Stannard in, and could I speak with him? She would let him in and summons my dad. When Dad stepped into the room, and she was gone, he burst out a muffled greeting, "Hey Georgie, you old son of a bitch! Can I get a ride with the snakes to collect my bounty?" Off they went, laughing, and sharing stories of old times.

Often times Jim would show up slightly intoxicated with the snakes in his bag, still alive. In order to get full benefit out of them, he had stopped off at "The Flame Eaters grill," throw the rattling bag on the bar, and asked for drinks. Charlie styles would always eagerly oblige.

It wasn't uncommon for Andy to be seen "bumming" a ride here and there, but a few weeks before his death he was seen walking toward town and into N.Y. state, not hitchhiking. We learned later that he had walked all the way to brother Henry's home in Glens Falls, N.Y. which was where he later passed away.

Several weeks passed before my father and uncle found the courage to walk the 150 yards south of the farmhouse to do Andy the courtesy of closing out the cabin and dealing with his affects. Kids in tow, they finally picked a time that felt right and next door we went, not expecting any surprises. As we followed behind Dad and Uncle Ed, I noticed that they had both curiously stopped about ten feet from the door, long faces and some hesitation.

As I approached, grabbing dad's shirt-tail for security, I read something on Andy's slate that I recall as vividly today as that day in 1957. It said, "Be it ever so humble, there's no place like home." Signed "Andrew H Howard."

CHAPTER SEVEN

LIKE FATHER LIKE SON

ANDY WAS A GREAT INFLUENCE on my father and a close friend to my grandfather. All three had great influence on me, but not until I was an adult did I give much thought to how generational influence works, or in how many ways.

My grandfather was a man of very few words. The entry into his diary on November 17, 1910 was, simply, "George was born today." For each of all three days of a blizzard in another year, his one word entry was "snow." There were hundreds of one word entries to those journals that recorded his life. Only things of importance like his lumber camp and his horses earned more wordy entries into his record.

With each generation, the entries got more involved. I'm not sure what that says about "generational influence," but it is nonetheless, in my family, true. A January 1, 1930 entry by my father said, "Scripture killed our pig today which weighed 258 pounds. He did not steal any of the liver. I held the beast while Scripture stabbed him. Father, Ed and I took him to the state line to have him dressed, and then got him in the afternoon. Both trips were made in the old Ford." Probably the same pig mentioned in grandfather's diary July 15, the previous year. "Andy and I got a pig from Ed Bigelow today." On January 29, he wrote "We spent most of the day up in the woods. At night, we listened to 'Coon' Sanders orchestra. I stalled the Caterpillar tractor twice today." Then comes my generation. Throughout my twenties numerous entries to my diaries used whole pages to describe the family gatherings at my grandmother Phelps' house, and told lengthy stories of other recorded days. But honestly, my grandmother's baked leg of lamb followed by ice cream with her homemade chocolate sauce deserved a whole page.

My grandfather Stannard was a very busy and successful businessman in the pre-depression era, with two farms, a grist mill in town, sawmill on the home farm, and lumber camp in the north woods housing up to 28 men and a cook, Mrs. Jackson, who came and went to prepare meals. He raised cattle, sheep and a huge annual potato crop. He manufactured and sold grain and lumber, sold wool, potatoes and firewood. He supplied the "entire" town with firewood, and donated all of what was needed to heat "all" of the churches. My father said that in August, both sides of Inman Pond Road for about one mile, back toward the Sheldon Farm, was lined with four-foot-long, split, firewood, piled 6'-8' high, waiting to be sawed, stove lengths and delivered to town. His friends and neighbors, the Reed family were well known local teamsters who transported most of it to town on lumber wagons pulled by beautiful teams of horses. Dad recalled the regular Saturday afternoon meetings he attended with Grandfather where teamsters, woodsmen, farm hands all gathered around to collect their pay for the week, after which they exited on "riled up" horses, noisily racing each other toward town for a wild evening of barroom banter, wrestling matches and occasional group fights in the park, for entertainment.

One group included "One eyed Jim," "One eared Jim," and "Jim." There was "Axe handle Jones," "Billy Chicken," Turkey Bristol," "Chauncey Sharp," "Scripture," "Plynn," and "Doom." Then there was "Wee Pelkey" who ate raw meat sandwiches and rode all kinds of half wild animals, bare-back. There was also a darker sounding character by the name of "Flea Beebe" who rode several horses to their deaths by trying to "jump them" over things like the cannon in the park, and following the Fourth of July parade each year attempted to jump one over the river at the foot of Main Street Hill. There was one other group, Dad referred to as "Red, Ed, Ned, Fred, Ted, and Butch." The stories are endless and mostly hilarious. I could write a separate book about them, and perhaps someday, I shall.

So, Andy taught my father how to hunt and fish, pick apples and berries and tree nuts by the bushel, cut wood and do barn chores. He was, in addition to an employee, a sort of trusted family babysitter at times, and home schooler.

The stories my father told about Andy were endless and the resulting intrigue lured me to the outdoors to learn it all and learn to appreciate nature and all its bounty. Andy hunted and fished every day. My father hunted and fished every chance he got, and so do I. Andy was a trapper. My father learned that trade and taught it to me at an early age. From the age of twelve to about 18 my friend Rick and I ran extensive trap lines up and down the full length of Mud Brook from the "Marsh" to the river at "Ranney's Rocks," and in beaver swamps and fox dens north of town. Running trap lines doubled as hunting trips for whatever was in season, rabbits, squirrels, partridge, ducks, geese, etc. and our mothers prepared it all for the dinner table, including an outrageous squirrel pie with dumplings.

Successful day of deer hunting on the farm in 1930.

John Roberts on a good day of fishing. One caught by him, the other by the author's dad, George.

Andy and my grandfather taught Dad how to efficiently manufacture hundreds of cords of firewood annually, using the best equipment and methods of that day. Each of them were in the firewood business more than 50 years and I have been, as well. My dad could de-limb one side of a felled hardwood tree with the "sharp side" of a double bit axe when he was 50, faster than a man with a chainsaw could finish the other side. He could split firewood with the "dull side," as fast as a good man with a two-way wood splitter, while laughing in a loud high-pitched voice that could be heard a mile away. He taught me to use both sides of the axe efficiently before I was 10, and I loved it but warn your 21st century kids and grandkids not to try this at home. Beginning in 1980 through 1985, following a disappointing business partnership and ultimate failure, I made my good living, raised five kids, and paid off my debts by producing roughly 600 cords of hardwood firewood annually, using a chainsaw and a six pound, single bit, "Rail splitter" axe, and delivered it, loaded and unloaded by hand to retail customers everywhere, including Killington ski resort area in a worn out, beefed up, 1978 Ford truck, one cord at a time, two or more times a day, most days, six or seven days a week. Let me just add that during those years, I was one of the toughest "Sons of a bitches" you'd ever meet. I was healthy, happy, and almost impervious to reality!! Could life get better than that? Depends on how better is defined.

Author chunking firewood in 1980.

My wonderful and amazing wife, Kath, helped me buy a new and bigger delivery truck, and bought me a four-way wood splitter to break the seemingly unconscious spell I was in in 1985 and we used them to put our company, Wood One, Inc. on the map with annual productions of as high as 1300-1400 cords, and to go on to start other business ventures, expand our holdings, raise kids, and in general, defy the odds! I owe this woman everything, and with her, life has been so very, very good!!

Suddenly they were building wood splitters that I couldn't keep up with an ax. So, it's apparent to me that generational influences and inherited traits and memory rule the day.

My grandfather survived similar struggles in his working career. A once wealthy farmer, logger, and businessman, and wool producer of some notoriety, he lost his entire fortune in the market crash of 1929 and subsequent loss of business activity through the 1930's. In the thirties, now in his 60's, his relatives and children fought hard, and successfully to save his farms and most of his real estate. My father, working a job for $21 a week, took groceries to his dad each week on payday and worked nights in his shop on the farm as a cabinet maker to pay taxes on the properties, and help his brother through med school. The result was that their hard work together allowed some property including the home farm to remain in the family. Dad used to say, "hard work never killed anybody" and "when the going is tough, the tough get going." When asked how he got through it all, he said, "It's no hill for a stepper."

Author's Dad in 1930, showing off the new wood delivery truck.

As for my dad's share of hardships, toward the end of his second year at Harvard in 1930, he received a western union from grandfather, instructing him to use that enclosed train fare to return home early from school and bring his belongings. Grandfather could no longer pay his tuition. He followed instructions, packed his belongings, returned home on the train and spent the next three years in lumber camp, felling and de-limbing trees, chopping, splitting and stacking four-foot firewood and living on potatoes, peanut butter, bread and lard. Few in my generation have experienced the hardships and disappointments of some folks in those times, but future generations will again, and probably worse. That "Greatest generation" survived the Depression, and World War One, World War Two and Korea. Only a handful of people alive today can describe that struggle for and the intense cost of freedom and capitalism. That struggle and its ultimate success defined our nation and our state until about the 1970's. Hopefully soon, something will be awakened in the spirits of Vermonters and all Americans that will regain what has been lost since then. That idle strength can rebuild America, and hopefully will, when the time is right.

Seeing the troops off to fight World War I from Fair Haven, Vermont Train Depot.

MADE IN VERMONT

World War I Fair Haven, Vermont reserve unit at Park.

Speaking more of "Inherited memory" on a nice October day in 1990, I went for a walk in the family wood lot, looking for deer sign, and smelling the clean, crisp smells of the fall woods. I walked around the south end of the pond as geese trumpeted their nervous exit. I felt bad having disturbed their solitude. I was on the roadway that circled the pond and wound its way up past the "Big Rock" onto the oak ridge. I'd walled it a hundred times or more. This day, I was drawn away from the road to check out a huge hemlock tree about three feet in diameter and a hundred feet high, uncharacteristic of that area, both in species, and size. I walked up the hill on the south side of the road about forty feet to the tree and put one hand on it while I looked up into its impressive height. Afterwards I turned around, put my back against the tree and relaxed while looking over the pond to the other side where grandfather's sawmill once operated. Suddenly, the hair stood straight on my neck and a very cold, almost crippling chill came over my body causing goose bumps more intense than any I had felt before. It lasted far too long and offering no explanation, I thought I should leave. But what was it? Was something watching me? I looked all around as far as I could see and nothing was there. Just birds and squirrels and a beaver on the pond. Suddenly as strangely as the feeling had overtaken me, a scene developed in my mind, as if in a dream. It was as if I was now my father, standing under that tree sixty years or more earlier. I could envision the mill operating next to the brook that had not yet become a pond. Sounds, sights, and smells overtook me that were from another time. Shocked at what I had imagined, the goose bumps returned, and as I reflected on the experience and readied myself to leave, I seemed to suddenly see a blanket on the ground, under the tree, with Grandmother Stannard and my fathers' young sisters having a picnic on it. Totally freaked out I left the tree and never returned to it. I believe to this day that I was experiencing the mystery of what I call "inherited memory, something that can likely only occur when a combination of circumstances exist that will allow it, or in a dream.

I didn't think about that tree much after that for a while, until Bill, a member of my logging crew came out of the woods a few years later with that tree behind our log skidder. As the goose bumps returned briefly, I realized that I should have told the crew not to cut that tree, but later it occurred to me other trees like that one will survive the logging, and still others that I have stood under for hours hunting and reflecting, and that in fifty years or more, some of my progeny will stand under one of them and experience a similar phenomenon. Life is not only good, but perhaps transferable through memory.

CHAPTER EIGHT

FLIGHT HISTORY

A YOUNG BOY, EAGER TO FLY, and dreaming of becoming a pilot someday, showed up at the airport in Fair Haven on a sunny June morning, ready and eager to make his case. "Will you take me up today Mr. Council? Please take me up! I want to fly!" "Do you have the two bucks yet young man? I've got a few older guys ahead of you, and you are pretty young."

Head down and frowning, Dick answered, "No sir, Mr. Council, but I sure want to fly." Apparently, the instructor saw something in that boy and offered a potential solution. "Tell you what, Dicky, I'm going to be a little short on gas today. Here's two five gallon cans and a couple bucks. Bring back the change and the cans, full of gas, by the time I need them, and I'll take you up when I'm done. It's a good half mile or more to Joe Bird's Garage, so don't dilly dally." The 10-

year-old boy was all smiles and legs as he raced away with the cans, on foot to the station nearly a mile away, in town. Sometime later he returned with the heavy cans full of gas, for that first ride and lesson that would lead to a lifelong career in flight.

The boy was my friend Rick's Dad, who would enter the air corps for WWII, become a B-29 pilot flying missions over Europe. He would return to Fair Haven in 1945 to begin his career as a small business owner while struggling to study to become a commercial pilot. After completion of that task, while raising a family he accepted an invitation to become a business partner in a charter flight business and guide service to Canadian destinations based out of Burlington, making regular seaplane flights into and out of remote destinations in the provinces. Then he would open a flight instruction school, and together with partners would soon develop a small commercial airline company that would include regular mail routes to places like Boston and Chicago. The name of that company was Air North, that would develop into a much larger company, "Northern Airways" based out of Burlington, and several other ports. Eventually they would sell out to Mohawk Airlines, also then based out of Burlington, and larger ports across the country.

As a retirement challenge, Dick would contract himself out to Exxon Oil, as a Bush pilot in Libya, exploring and mapping potential new oil fields, for five years. He would return to buy property on the Lamoille River in Essex, where he could commute by sea plane, then more property in Alaska and ultimately half interest in the Big Lake Airport, outside Wasilla.

In my early years, he was my flight instructor at Fair Haven, and by the time we were sixteen, Rick and I had more solo hours than we needed for pilot licenses.

Dick was a man with a huge broad smile, an eager attitude toward life and challenges, and a presence that couldn't be denied. I remember in that summer of my tenth year, flying stalls, and upside-down maneuvers that scared me to death until I learned to control them myself. I had ample confidence in Dick's capabilities and apparently my mother did as well, since she never questioned me when I announced I was headed to the airport with Dick and Ricky for a day of flying.

Life was so damn good!!

That earlier instructor was Merrit Council, who was later rumored to have instructed more young pilots pre-WWII than any other traveling instructor in America. He must have been good at it since all of the pilots from Fair Haven, most if not all, trained by Council, returned to Fair Haven after the war, decorated, celebrated, and mostly intact. Fair Haven's notable WWII pilots included Brig, Gen. Edwin L. Little, Clement Tomasi, Col. Tom Perry, and others that I knew less well. My father was the only one trained by Council that saw limited WWII flight in the Air Corp, as he was transferred at the army's discretion to the engineers and sent to Saipan. Ironically, flights couldn't land there until somebody built airports for them to land on.

Life was precious. Life in the free world was in jeopardy, and the lives lived and lost by that amazing generation of heroes is responsible for the existence of ours!

I remember a day in deer hunting season, in the late 1950's, when my grandfather Phelps and Clem Tomasi, after several libations at the Fair Haven Hotel bar that morning, loaded Clem's plane to fly a mission over the North Woods bombing their Legion buddies with bags of flour, on their organized hunt there in the afternoon. Numerous times I recall Clem and Grandfather Phil buzzing the outskirts of town, flying under the power lines and performing numerous other tricks and stunts at low altitudes. They weren't crazy. They just drank a lot, and to them, life was only worth what you got out of it.

The airport was the Fair Haven Municipal Airport, one of only two municipal airports in Vermont, and at that time, one of very few anywhere. The 140 acre or so farm that the airport was on was given to the town to be used specifically for that purpose. All of those accomplished pilots were trained there. Airmail was transported in and out of town beginning on May 19, 1938. Among my late grandfather Phil Phelps' belongings still in the family possession is the first air mailed letter, sent out on that day to his friend in Middlebury, who later air mailed it back to him in Fair Haven.

Along with the loss of Vermont's economic vibrance and productive attitudes, went the disappearance of one of Fair Haven's most important assets, the Municipal Airport. After myself and several others on the airport committee worked successfully for years to secure 3.5 million dollars of federal grant money to upgrade and expand the airport, the voters turned down the towns $75,000 share to secure the money, and the select board shut the place down! History will shake its head on that decision. I cried!

CHAPTER NINE

FLIGHT HISTORY OF THE WORLD

IN AN AUGUST 12, 1931 letter to my dad from his old Harvard roommate and best friend, John Roberts, John wrote "Possibly you saw in the paper that Lindberg was here before he took off for Japan. We saw the whole works! He took off from Goose Rock Light, up the thorofare towards North Haven. We were anchored by the narrows to watch, near where we got soaked earlier. Lindy took off right in front of us!!!

That paragraph, matter-of-factly inserted into the middle of a two-page nonsense letter from the Roberts "Eastholm" in Vinal Haven, Maine in 1931 shows the contrast of looking at history in the making, and examination of its importance 85 years later.

I added this chapter to do just that, look back at perhaps the single most important event in American History. The rapid rise of the significance of flight in the growth of our economy, mobility, and defense capabilities defining us as a world power, at the top of the food chain, so to speak, and as defender of freedom and personal liberties at home and abroad. Folks like the Wright Brothers, Charles Lindberg and others played key roles in the development of our history, and the man who wrote those words to my dad, would go on to become one of them.

So many folks, like my dad and virtually all of his friends were interested in the concept and opportunities of flight in its early development. It was not unlike the attention given to the invention of computers and the resulting growth of the "tech" industry.

So many interesting occurrences entered the life of John Roberts as he embarked on what would become his career, above the ground that men had previously only walked on for millenniums. Life for John and others like him was interesting and exhilarating! My dad told me when he retired it was said that he had logged more commercial flight hours than any United pilot. His career began at Boeing school, and nine months of training known as the master pilot course that consisted of 924 hours of ground school, which included meteorology, navigation, engines, air, and business law, construction of planes, air traffic management and a host of lots of other important things. Then he was required to log 50 hours duel, and 154 hours solo. In contrast, when Ricky and I trained, our requirement for a simple non-commercial private license was 300 hours of flying. His included blind flying (with a hood over the cockpit) but also things like aerial surveying and photography. If that's not complete, what is?

They used five types of planes ranging from a small two seater trainer to an eight-place monoplane and the then famous Boeing Mail Plane, which was a big bi-plane with a 500 HP Pratt and Whitney Hornet engine. His December 18,1931 Christmas card to my dad was printed by Boeing with a picture of the Boeing 203 primary trainer.

Another post card from him advertising "SHURETOURS" featured an American Airlines "Flagship Fleet" twin engine passenger plane. The ad read "Live a lot and like it... In a 200 mile an hour "room with a view." Surprisingly there's no sensation of height, or speed. You feel no connection with the earth except as an exalted spectator."

A letter dated May 14, 1932 described "a number of interesting things going on at the airport yesterday." He described the arrival of the "Akron overhead." It apparently had a tough time getting there and had been expected for days. "It's based at Sunnyvale, a little bit south of here, so we got to see quite a lot of it." "Gosh, it's so big!" "Everybody who owned a ship around here had to go alongside to have a peek at the flying mountain. Twelve planes around it looking like so many flies."

"There were hordes of planes and people mussing around the airport all day to see it, including an Autogiro, Sikorsky twin engine boat, and an English Flying Boat." "The English boat belongs to a young Jap who is going to fly the Pacific in it in the next few weeks. He brought it over from England and had it assembled in United's experimental hanger." "The Jap is backed by a Tokyo newspaper and isn't such a bad sort at all." "He's not bad looking for his type, speaks fair English, but better German, but he does hand out a laugh, for he tests out his ship wearing a derby at all times."

The boat is a Saunders-Roe with a Siddeley Lynx 200 HP motor." He expects to complete the distance in four hops, and will be acclaimed as the Japanese Lindbergh when he gets there.

Life for these guys was interesting and challenging, to say the least, but without their persistence, experimentation and daring, inventiveness and hard work, ours would be a much different world today. On any clear day now I can look up and see several huge jets leaving crisscrossing vapor steams, each carrying hundreds of passengers at speeds greater than that travelled by sound. To destinations, worldwide, counted by hours not days. I remember the first time I flew in a Piper Comanchee upside down. I remember the first single vapor stream I saw in the lonely sky and watched till it disappeared.

I remember the deafening rumble of the B-52 flying a few hundred feet over town at the close of the Vietnam War captained by a proud pilot, Tony Foley from here in town. Then somewhere, intermingled into all this amazing history, there was once an American space program, where John F. Kennedy's dream became everybody's and I remember the night at Fort Warren Drive In when "Beano" Benford stopped the movie, shut down the sound reel, and came on the mike to announce that if we stepped out of our cars and looked up to the eastern sky we would see "Sputnik" going over. I forgot which movie was playing.

On the beach in Maine, just before "Col. Charlie's" take off on his famous "Northern Route" flight to Japan.
Taken by John Roberts

Assumed to be unidentified Lindbergh family members with "Col. Charlie's" plane, near North Haven Main Residence.
Taken by John Roberts

CHAPTER TEN

SNAKE COUNTRY

FAIR HAVEN IS KNOWN FOR ITS RATTLESNAKES and points north of our airport is rattlesnake country. I was raised. as my father was, in the heart of rattlesnake country. I live today on the original Stannard family farm settled by my ancestor, Samuel in 1780. The farm exists on the southernmost end of "The Great Ledge," aka "Rattlesnake Ridge."

My father was still rattlesnake hunting for bounty, from time to time, when I was a kid, a passion for him that soon faded away as snake populations declined a great deal, Rattlesnake by-products became less popular, and ultimately the bounty was removed.

All I knew about them in my youth was that they rattled, that they were a stunningly beautiful velvet black in July, after shedding, and that bounty money bought baseballs, .22 shells, and fishing equipment. My dad knew right where they were, all the time. Curiosity generally convinced me to tag along on most of his outdoor escapades and snake hunts were no exception. My only recollections were at a very early age from about seven to ten years old, but I learned a lot and remembered it. I recall his saying that often repeated, "Look high in the fall, and low in the spring." I guess the theory was that they went into the upper ledges in the fall and worked their way down into them, coming out low in the spring. When folks talk about "Dens," one gets the impression that there's one entry or exit, or cave-like structure where the snakes enter and exit. Actually, they enter the ledges at various random points in somewhat condensed areas of rock ledge crevices, and winter somewhere below the frost line, exiting at convenient points somewhere below in the spring. Places known by locals as "The Main Den" and "South Den" are simply points of concentration where it is easiest to find snakes at certain times of the year. We would drive to the Proctor Farm at the foot of "Long Hill" in late April and from there enter the woods into wet areas below the ledges. There, by some method known to my dad, that I never could copy with great success, he would find snakes, as many as ten or fifteen on a morning hunt. At that time of year, the snakes were interested in sun and where the sun hit the rocks, they would curl up on boulders and hang from ledge faces warming themselves. He told me that rattlers gave live birth to their young, but were pregnant with them up to four years, only giving birth after building a certain amount of fat, a direct result of the amount of sun they receive. Little ones are born over winter, with one rattle, and will grow one new rattle each year for their lifetime.

He taught me the "Two thumbs rule." You never approached a coiled snake, but you could easily put a stretched-out snake at ease and pick it up behind the head leaving no more room behind the base of the head than the width of two thumbs. Again, school your 21st century kids not to try this at home.

I learned early on how to "aim the snake at the gun." He used a .32 caliber revolver with brass shotgun loads. He would make the snake coil, then at three lengths and at arm's length, turn the gun in slow steady circles, until the snakes' concentration followed it. After pulling the trigger he would say, "Oh look at that, the snake shot itself!"

The rattles can break off. There were stories of disgruntled neighbors, breaking the rattles off and letting the snakes go in well placed locations, to even up a score against animals or even people. Even today, I know of at least one prankster who does it randomly just to be funny.

Ironically, preservation groups today try to protect this species and habitat with little success. The same groups who purchase lands to create preserves, also don't believe in cutting trees or cropping fields, which has removed needed sunlight from the equation. One conservation effort interferes greatly with the others, and I predict the ultimate extinction of our local Timber Rattlesnake Chapter.

CHAPTER ELEVEN

TRIBUTE TO PATRIOTS

THIS BOOK HAS BEEN THE RESULT OF my best effort to describe the unique contributions of everyday native Vermonters in the development of a free state and free country and the unique characteristics of "Vermontism" that give these people and places identity and unique history. I've described as best I can the evolution of native Vermonters, through my relationships and associations with them over seventy strangely metamorphic years of history here.

My ancestors and so many others left behind a legacy of drive and determination, sacrifice and strength of character, and constructive results perhaps taken too much for granted or not adequately appreciated by a struggling new Millennial generation." Vermont, in my lifetime has changed from the most conservative state in the union to the most liberal, a highly productive manufacturing and agricultural mecca, to an industrial ghost town of sorts. From a poster of liberty, individual free thinking of its people and the autonomy of its towns, to a bureaucratic socialist state. The God given rights of its people have been taken away by the state sold back to them in the form of licenses, permits and fees by un-elected "officials." I'll let the reader be the judge of which system was or is better for the people in the present or the future, but always bear in mind that all of those who fought in our bloody wars past and present, fought for constitutionally, God given, natural rights of a free people. For me that fight is best described in a letter dated October 28, 1861, to my great grandfather, E.H. Phelps, by Charles Emmet Abel, aka "Abe" (enlisted 09/04/61 5GT Company H of the 5th Vermont Infantry). He penned the letter to Phelps, a Middlebury College classmate and also an Orwell, VT native. The letter was in regard to the death of a mutual friend, from Orwell, John LaMountain of Company H of the 5th VT, whose war records indicate that he died on the same date as the letter.

Describing his disease, death, absence from roll call at camp Griffin, VA. in the morning, and a nighttime burial, he wrote:

"In the stillness of the autumn evening when the day has given way to darkness, and the stars alone of the heavenly spheres watched over our solemn proceedings, when all the natural world seemed to impress upon our minds the often hinted fact that all things having a beginning must also have an end, we placed the remains of poor John in its' grave, by the side of a pretty grove, to mingle his dust with the soil of the enemy, which are now alike but with this exception. His was the dust of freedom, while that in which it is now moldering lies, is tainted with the foul curse of slavery."

Camp of 15th Cavalry at Manchester Center, Vermont.

Soon after my great grandfather Phelps received that letter, he petitioned his Congressman and received a clerkship in the Paymasters Dept. at Hilton Head, South Carolina. In the dialog, less controversial in that day, he wrote, "This is a terrible southern place, sandy and fearfully hot." "Niggers and soldiers comprise almost the entire population." Serving as paymaster under Col. P. E. Dye, he described in his diary, listening to the shelling at night, and then visiting Charlestown the day after its fall, to pay troops as they were re-directed or sent home. He described the faces of despair on the soldiers and solemn demeanor of survivors on several pages of his diary.

MADE IN VERMONT

On another occasion, he described sleeping on the floor of a riverboat traveling to another gathering of troops in need of pay. He described that night as "A living hell. It was by far, the coldest I've ever been."

The day after Lincoln's assassination, he entered that "Word was received in camp today of the death of our President Abraham Lincoln." Then in his papers were the minutes of a meeting held two weeks later at Hilton Head to discuss the design of the monument there honoring the felled president.

Phelps was an interesting character, and not just a Civil War traveling Paymaster with saddle sores. Before the war he was a teacher. During and after the war he was a somewhat accomplished poet. Also throughout the war he was a reporter serving the Fair Haven papers and the Rutland Herald.

Phelps was born in Ticonderoga, N.Y. on January 16th, 1839. At the age of two he moved to Orwell, VT where he grew up working his grandfather's farm and attending the District School until he was 16. Between then and Civil War duty he attended Brandon Seminary formerly Vermont Literary and Scientific Institution, Then Shoreham Academy in Shoreham to prepare for his attendance at Troy Conference Academy (now known as Green Mountain College), in Poultney, VT. In 1857, he was admitted to Middlebury College as a freshman, graduating in 1861.

With a reputation as one of the best writers in the college, he gained notoriety as a poet, much of his work eventually published. After Middlebury, he began teaching in his home town, and a family school until he answered the call of the Civil War. As a clerk and Paymaster serving under Col. PE. Dye, he served at Hilton Head S.C., Florida, Georgia and numerous other points until May 1865. Then he did special duty in New York City, Albany and Buffalo until in December 1865, he was ordered to Denver, Colorado territory, while in that duty he visited nearly all the forts and military posts, and claimed to have seen very much of the western life of that time. He served the dual role of a reporter throughout his tenure.

Upon eventual return to Fair Haven and Orwell, he became an officer of Fair Haven's First National Bank, co-owner of the Fair Haven Clock Co., partner in Fair Haven Marbleized Slate Products, and ultimately trustee of Middlebury College, and a sheep farmer.

It's very hard for anyone in 2016 to feel what it took to leave your home, family and income not necessarily expecting to return and travel thousands of miles across your own country by foot, horseback, trains and boats to fight the cold and starvation, in a war that featured hand to hand combat against people that look like your own. So-called Americans who would apologize for this country's defense of freedom and the principals of personal liberty, unencumbered by any government, or those who would consider burning the American flag should be enlisted to similar duty, and a few more hours of history lessons.

Our founders afforded us the liberty to experience the fruits of this suffering, loss and hardship, but conversely charged us with the responsibility to guard and defend it with all our resources, now, and in future.

I am also fortunate to be descended from three patriots that were active members of Ethan Allen's "Green Mountain Boys," a semi-civilized group of very tough and smart patriots responsible for winning several skirmishes and battles that led to victory in the Revolution, and for saving the territory of Vermont from claims by bordering states. Perhaps the subjects of another book. Life for them was doggedly committed to the call of freedom and democracy, and their blood and sweat still flows from those who fight to carry on their legacy.

CHAPTER TWELVE

BEAUROCRATIC SOCIALISM

EVEN THOUGH BORN IN THE 1940's, folks in my generation are called," products of the 60's. Televisions, rock and roll, muscle cars, paid vacations, cannabis, free love, the controversial war! good jobs, good money, good drugs, good health care, and best of all, we were all still free!! Factories flourished, the Eisenhower highway system was built, goods and services were in high demand at home and abroad. Agriculture was mechanizing, thriving, and growing more things and more of them, through chemistry. America was feeding, policing and protecting the world. The world was shrinking. Then by around 1970, Woodrow Wilson's "progressive" philosophies became a communicable disease in Vermont, and Vermont of all unlikely places, began its leadership role in the development of a growing national "liberalism." Republican Governor Deane Davis got the ball rolling with a hugely controversial new land development law known as "Act 250," which led to the eventual control of all land use in Vermont and even an Environmental court system, that some would argue betrayed all principals of constitutional law and became the father of a new phenomenon invented by me known as "Bureaucratic socialism." Predictions of its result were conflicting. Some thought it's so called "10 acre" loophole would encourage development to take place by expanding community centers where connectivity to services like water, sewer, power, and transportation were close by. Others predicted that the entire state would be covered with homes and businesses spread out a quarter mile apart, forced to provide their own services to avoid permit review. Low and behold, over time municipalities drastically increased property taxes to cover increasing costs of providing services to a limited market and rural development slowed, due to increasingly restrictive and cost prohibitive permit processes so both predictions failed, any development slowed, and Vermont's economy slumped! Vermont's economy shrunk as the government grew. The government was cheating its' people and the people were starting to cheat the government. Banks were deregulated and started screwing the people and people started screwing the banks. The banks struggled, the people struggled, the government grew and stressed itself to bail out both. What a country!!

As the decades passed and ethics and morality deteriorated, the developing educational bureaucracy began the "Dumbing down" of America. The government carried out a process of

MADE IN VERMONT

"Dumbing down" the country's economics. The goal of education became "mediocrity" rather than "exceptionalism." The economic goals of government became "mediocrity. The government and the Federal Reserve partnered up to develop the "dumbing down of the nation's economy" and a slump into economic mediocrity. The increasingly liberal politics produced by all of this, resulted in the "dumbing down" of government, at all levels, and by 2015 Vermont led the country as the dumbest place in American to live and work, and the country started bouncing off "Rock bottom," as a leader and example to the world.

Vermont's greatest contribution to the "Liberalization" of America was sending a series of glory seeking, self-promoting creeps to Washington, looking for careers at something with a lifetime guarantee, wealth, power, and no requirement whatsoever for accomplishment. The oath they took to uphold the Constitution became nothing more than a false formality. The only thing Vermont should be thankful for is that they don't accomplish anything and that they certainly won't under eight years of the possibility of a president Donald Trump, and that they will all be too old to recover from it afterwards.

My criticisms of the Vermont delegation may sound a little harsh, but my opinions, over time, have been shaped, other than by the obvious, by stories and information presented to me by personal friends involved at high levels of federal service, some of it "classified," at the time.

For example, consider the one about King Hussein's funeral. President Clinton, facing an impeachment vote, calls Vermont's Patrick Leahy, and invites him to attend the funeral with him on

Air Force One. In flight, Clinton explains to the senator that he desperately needs a Republican vote against his impeachment. He is aware of a "Dossier" held by Larry Flynn against Vermont's other illustrious Senator, Jim Jeffords regarding his marital improprieties and series of resulting spousal difficulties and offers fellow Democrat Leahy several things in return for Jeffords' vote, not the least of which is a huge payment of over budget transportation funding toward Vermont's ailing infrastructure.

Needless to say, the king was buried, the dossier was buried, the truth was buried, and among other "Perks" to Leahy, then state treasurer and former Governor Jim Douglas received a check in excess of 85 million dollars on behalf of the state in unexpected transportation funding. Sure enough, Jeffords had cast the only Republican "NO" vote and changed parties, fearing reprisal.

Now go back and see if you can count the ethics violations in that accounting. The only innocent player was state treasurer Jim Douglas. If I sound like a skeptic, perhaps someone can tell me why the media has never disclosed the fact that five cargo ships, <u>flying no flags</u>, were anchored together in the Red Sea, apparently hiding Saddam Hussein's WMD's, later sunk from underneath by Navy Seals. Perhaps the media was never informed either? What about Congress? Did they lie or were they lied to?

Or, I've always wondered why the Canadian Border was closed in the early AM on 911, hours in advance of the Twin Towers attack. I expect we'll never know, but was word out that something was up and no one in government responded??

I would suggest that the government that is supposed to be controlled by its people, has taken control of the people. There are some signs that America will catch a break and somewhat repair itself, but I would doubt that the same is in store for

Vermont anytime soon. Vermont has become a third world country, and Vermont would be wise to take the advice of its own George Aiken. He said, "You can destroy happiness by legislation, but you certainly cannot force it upon anybody by the same method."

The republic of Vermont faces greater difficulties than when three of my ancestors fought, without respect for their fate, with the Green Mountain Boys, for freedom from tyranny in the Revolutionary War. The American republic faces some of its greatest challenges since the Civil War. On April 4, 1865, Fair Haven's A.N. Adams wrote these words to my great grandfather, E.H. Phelps, "I want to inform you, after you have heard of it, that Richmond is ours! Ours and the Union's forever!" Hip, Hip, Hurrah! So much for young America. It will do to glory a little in our success after the costly struggle, but, really I cannot feel unalloyed enthusiasm in our victory, I cannot feel that the union is a fixed fact forever, tho' I do believe that Republican government is greatly strengthened and perpetuated on American soil. Perhaps there will not soon be another open rebellion, but we cannot cover the fact that our form of government, so rational and finest in conception, is terribly uncertain from other and unobserved causes. These presidential revolutions every four years will, I fear, one day destroy all the heroic achievements of this bloody war.

It seems ironic that in April of 2017, I am quoting Adams profound words of April 1865, and that the accuracy of his several statements offer such similarity to today's issues. Once again, a group of Americans feeling a disconnect with government and sense of urgency for change are celebrating a so-called "Republican victory," but with the unusual caveat that too much enthusiasm could be considered pre-mature. More than at any time in my life, I feel that the Union of America is no "fixed fact forever." I am an optimist, but find it increasingly difficult to remain optimistic about the survival of the "rational" ideals of our amazing founders.

It could also be said that this recent "Presidential Revolution" was the one that tore the country apart. I think it's deeper and far more complicated than that. I think it has been a process of gradual deterioration for forty to fifty years.

It is also ironic that so much attention is given to the alleged involvement of the Russians. In the Cold War years of the 1960's and 1970's, the Soviet Union often made the claim that they would eventually "take over the United States, without firing a shot. It was my feeling back then that their influence was at the forefront of step one of the "Dumbing down of our educational system and infiltration of socialist idealism into our universities. No Congressional hearings were held. I have briefly described the sequence of events that followed in previous chapters.

In 2017, America is engaged in the early stages of an, as yet undeclared Civil War. It won't be declared until the people finish choosing up sides. There are several complications. The far left and far right are one in the same. Mainstream Republicans and Democrats are dysfunctional. Moderates are a growing and helpless minority. Neither party has any real respect for historical constitutional continuity. If they did, there would be no national debt, none of the regressive forms of taxation would exist, health care would not be a "national right." Payroll deductions for social security and Medicare would be a "choice," no intervention into the affairs of other governments would ever take place, and "bureaucrat" would still be a dirty word. I could go on and on, but would rather suggest that American history be re-introduced, honestly into the educational system, which will not happen.

Washington D.C. is made up of 535 deadbeats, about 500 of whom are not honest or well-intended. Most of them are so old, they were usefully educated, but have forgotten what they learned. The rest are the victims of the effects of the entire dumbing down process. One party has become three parties and the other has coalesced and prepared for war. I believe that "Term limits" are the most important issue of the day.

To further complicate this tragic overthrow of decency and productivity, the body of 535 elected officials have, over decades, produced and authorized power and authority to tens of thousands of "unelected" officials (bureaucrats), who have now taken on a life of their own and are showing very disturbing signs of controlling the 535, and us.

Meanwhile, the media has chosen sides and declared war on each other and whichever party or groups they associate with the opposing side, the left side is in the streets rioting, the right is militarizing, and the 535 are "eating their own." As a native of Fair Haven, VT, USA, all I can say, perhaps devoid of "political correctness" is, God Bless Fair Haven, God Bless Vermont, and God Bless the USA.

T H E   E N D

References

Conant, Edward. *Conant's Vermont.* Edited by Mason S. Stone, Fifth ed. revised & enlarged, Tuttle Co., 1907.

MADE IN VERMONT

CHAPTER Thirteen

FUN WITH PICTURES

Evolution of Fair Haven Park and Goodrich Memorial Fountain.

Phil Stannard

Goodrich Memorial Fountain in Fair Haven Park.

MADE IN VERMONT

The Park and Fountain, Fair Haven, Vermont.

View along West Castleton "West Shore" Road of Lake Bomoseen, very early 20th century near Fair Haven, Vermont.

Along "East Shore" (now Vermont Route 30) of Lake Bomoseen, very early 20th century.

MADE IN VERMONT

West Castleton-"West Shore" Road along Lake Bomoseen, very early 20th century, near Fair Haven, Vermont.

Taking a break from haying to pose for a photo.

A serious business deal in "the works."

Fancy with four wheels and furs.

MADE IN VERMONT

Horse and driver, dressed to kill on Lake Bomoseen, Vermont.

Stylish winter travel – 1900.

Never mind the driver, LOOK AT ME!

OK, you walk, I'll ride in the carriage.

MADE IN VERMONT

Looks a little crowded, I'll wait here!

Who says the depot workhorse steam engine needs to look good?

Nursing class of 1912.

Together we can bridge "the great divide." The bridge at Carver's Falls went out in the Great Flood of 1927.

MADE IN VERMONT

"One of you say cheese, and the other one look annoyed."

Posing in the parking lot at the fair.

Phil Stannard

Let's do this, and head for the beer tent.

MADE IN VERMONT

Don't believe a damn thing she says.

Phil Stannard

Marianne Benford (teacher) and the entire enrollment of the Sheldon School in early twentieth century, located next door to the author's farm.

Posing at the woodpile. Sheldon School located at present site of Kevin and Eileen Durkee House, Sheldon Road, in Fair Haven, Vermont.

MADE IN VERMONT

Author's sons, Mike and Nate "Tapping the Sugarbush" in 21st century, just before the historic sap buckets are "outlawed" for commercial sugaring. "I rest my case!"